I0428040

Note From the Illustrator, Basak Tinli:

Fashion design process generally starts with inspiration then designers start to create by turning their inspirations into sketches. With the ability to draw their ideas, the garments start to take shape on paper. Fashion drawing is a very important step in studying fashion design. It is essential to have a nice presentation of your design before it comes to life. A good presentation can take a student to better schools, a designer to better job opportunities.

Today fashion industry is very complex and involves many different professions. Designers work together with stylists, make-up artists, hair dressers, photographers, models, merchandisers, manufacturers and illustrators. Many designers draw their own illustrations however within the fast paced system of the fashion industry, there is so little time to draw detailed illustrations. Every designer needs to find their own techniques of turning their ideas onto paper. These can include basic sketches, collages of the research done for a collection or technical drawings which paves the way for the pattern makers. The important thing is to be able to draw well to make their designs understood. While fashion illustrations show a designer's artistic ability at the first place sometimes fashion illustrators work alongside with them. Since the fashion illustration is the final product for the illustrator they can put more resources and time into creating fully detailed illustrations.

This book is designed as a resource book for fashion designers, fashion illustrators and students of fashion. There are 60 figure templates suitable for fashion design and designers can easily draw their own designs on the pose that will be best to show their design. Sketching over 9 head proportioned fashion figures makes it easier for designers to draw proportionally.
My purpose was to give many poses with various silhouettes. Poses from different angles like front view, back view, side view are included. While using this book you can trace or scan any pose then draw your own fashion design on it and then you can color them. Just remember these are stylized fashion figures and not for realistic anatomy. I hope each figure will be helpfull for your sketches and they will encourage you to create your own style while drawing them.

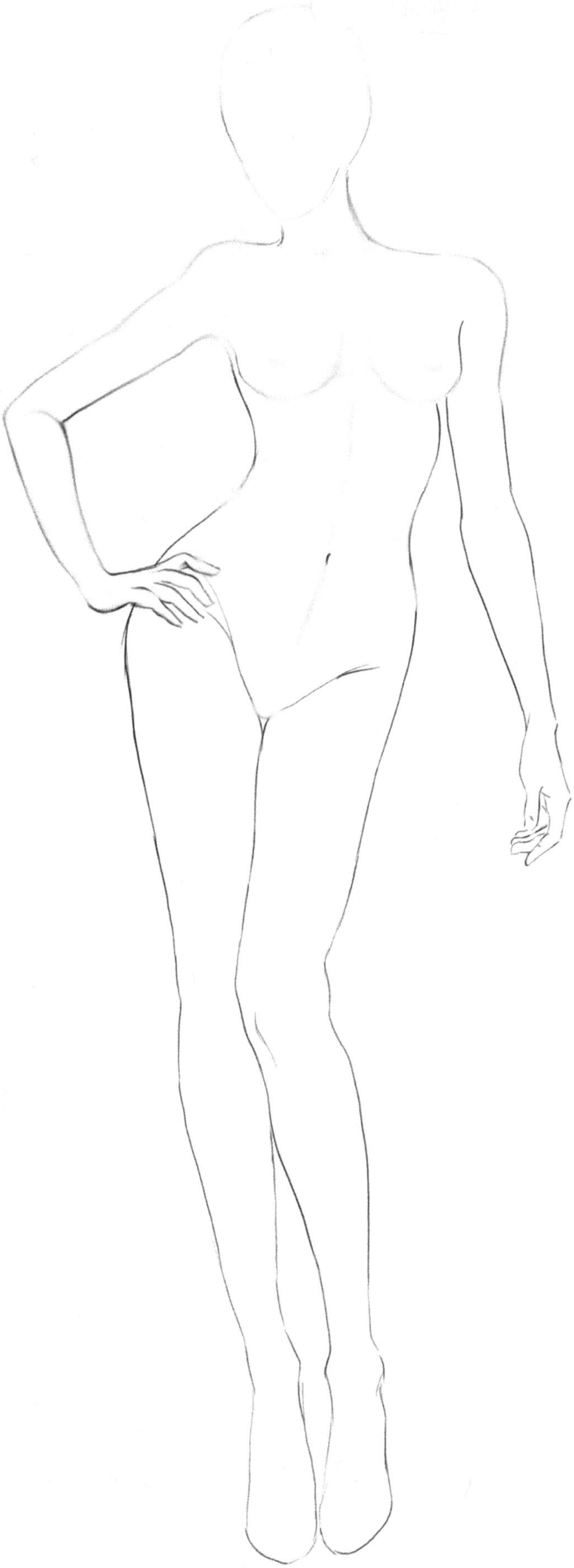

Proportions:

While the natural human figure can only be up to 8 heads, it is better to start drawing from 9 head proportions for fashion drawing. While using the templates in this book always remember that they are just guidelines and you can elongate the figures, alter their poses, emphasize body parts as you like.

Templates on the next page are base drawings showing the proportions used within this book. As a standard 9 head proportions are used for fashion design. However this is vaguely speaking because artists never limit themselves to rules when it comes to creativity. Many fashion illustrators use more elongated figures like 10 heads, 12 heads, any proportion they see fit to their desires.

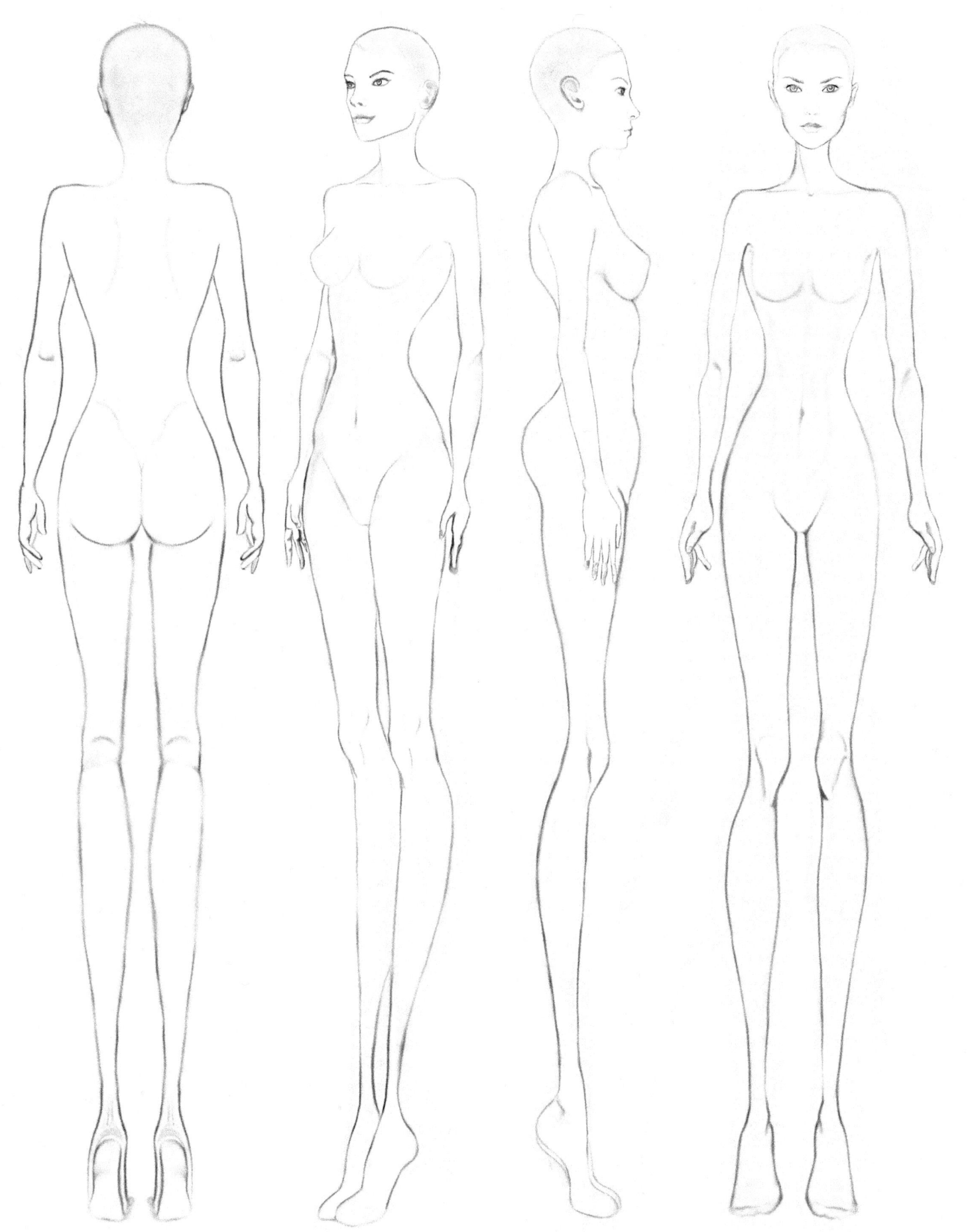

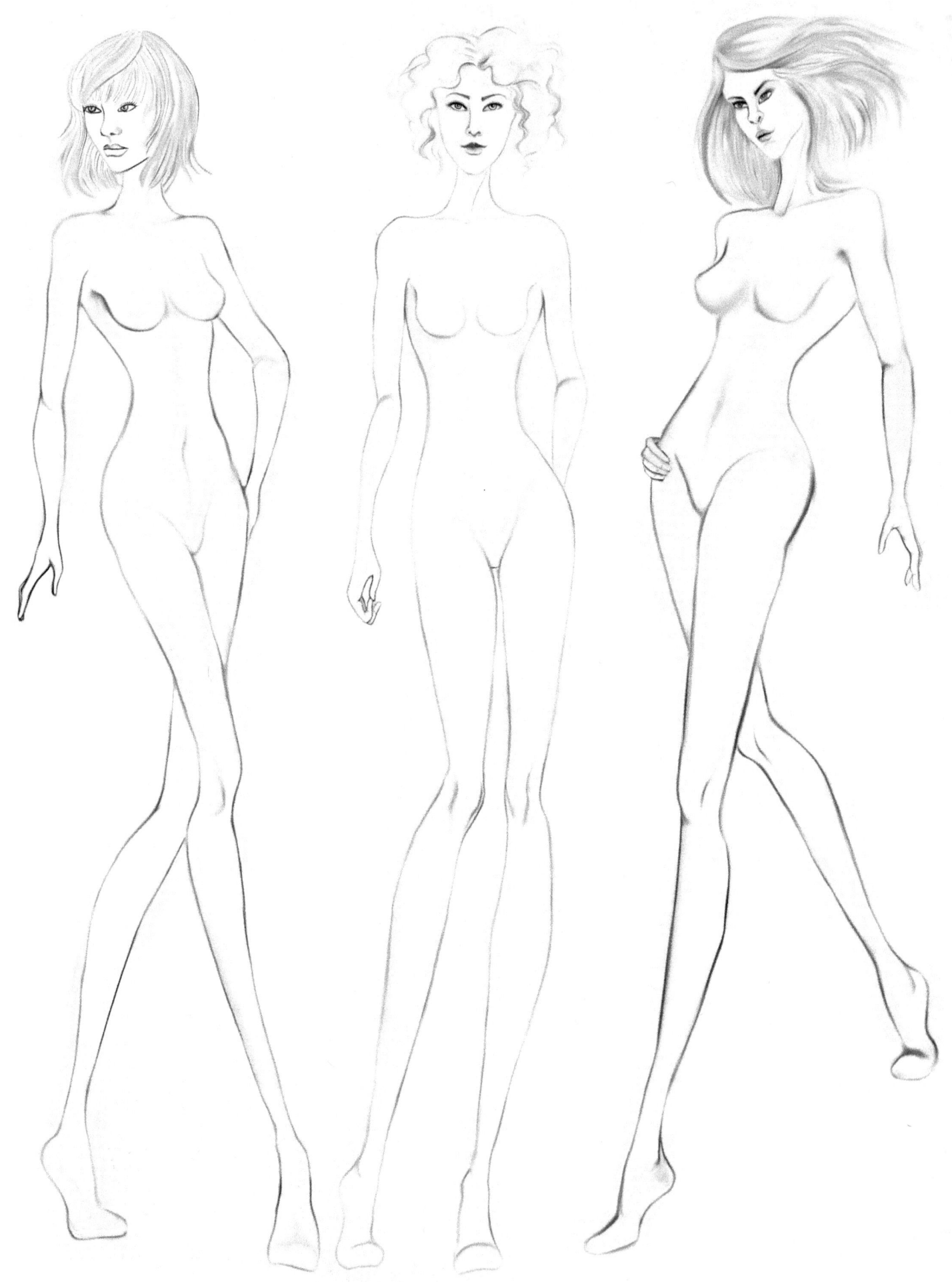

www.ingramcontent.com/pod-product-compliance
Lightning Source LLC
Chambersburg PA
CBHW081153290526
45795CB00008B/2901